50 Comfort Premium Dinner Dishes

By: Kelly Johnson

Table of Contents

- Classic Beef Wellington
- Maple-Glazed Salmon with Roasted Vegetables
- Herb-Crusted Prime Rib with Au Jus
- Truffle Butter Filet Mignon
- Bison Meatloaf with Garlic Mashed Potatoes
- Lobster Mac and Cheese
- Coq au Vin with Root Vegetables
- Wild Mushroom Risotto with Parmesan
- Braised Short Ribs with Red Wine Reduction
- Roasted Duck with Orange Glaze
- Garlic Butter Tomahawk Steak
- Seafood Chowder with Crispy Bacon
- Smoked Brisket with Maple Bourbon Glaze
- Classic Chicken Cordon Bleu
- Herb-Roasted Rack of Lamb
- Stuffed Pork Tenderloin with Apple and Cranberries
- Honey Dijon Glazed Ham
- Shrimp Scampi with Lemon Garlic Butter
- Slow-Cooked Osso Buco
- BBQ Glazed Meatloaf with Sweet Potato Mash
- Canadian Lobster Tail with Garlic Butter
- Stuffed Bell Peppers with Beef and Wild Rice
- Spaghetti Carbonara with Pancetta
- Buttermilk Fried Chicken with Biscuits
- Classic Chicken Alfredo
- Maple-Dijon Glazed Salmon
- Slow-Braised Lamb Shanks
- Pecan-Crusted Trout with Brown Butter
- Seared Scallops with Lemon Butter Sauce
- New York Strip Steak with Blue Cheese Butter
- Cajun Blackened Red Snapper
- Creamy Tuscan Chicken with Sun-Dried Tomatoes
- Wild Boar Ragu with Pappardelle
- Bacon-Wrapped Filet Mignon
- Garlic Butter Lobster Tails with Parmesan Asparagus

- Pan-Seared Duck Breast with Cherry Sauce
- Roast Chicken with Lemon and Thyme
- Seafood Paella with Saffron Rice
- Classic Shepherd's Pie
- Moroccan Spiced Lamb Chops
- Stuffed Shells with Ricotta and Spinach
- Sweet and Sour Glazed Pork Chops
- Blackened Cajun Salmon with Avocado Salsa
- Chicken Marsala with Creamy Mushroom Sauce
- Roasted Turkey with Cranberry Sauce
- Prime Rib with Horseradish Cream Sauce
- Creamy Lobster Bisque
- Beef Stroganoff with Egg Noodles
- Maple Glazed Duck Confit
- Lemon Garlic Shrimp Risotto

Classic Beef Wellington

Ingredients:

- 1 (2 lb) beef tenderloin
- 2 tbsp Dijon mustard
- 1/2 lb mushrooms, finely chopped
- 2 tbsp butter
- 2 tbsp shallots, minced
- 6 slices prosciutto
- 1 sheet puff pastry
- 1 egg, beaten

Instructions:

1. Sear tenderloin on all sides, then brush with Dijon mustard. Let cool.
2. Sauté mushrooms and shallots in butter until moisture evaporates. Let cool.
3. Lay prosciutto on plastic wrap, spread mushroom mixture over it, and place the beef on top. Roll tightly.
4. Wrap beef in puff pastry, sealing edges with egg wash. Chill for 30 minutes.
5. Bake at 400°F (200°C) for 25-30 minutes until golden brown. Let rest before slicing.

Maple-Glazed Salmon with Roasted Vegetables

Ingredients:

- 4 salmon fillets
- 1/4 cup pure maple syrup
- 1 tbsp Dijon mustard
- 1 tbsp soy sauce
- 1 lb mixed vegetables (carrots, Brussels sprouts, potatoes)
- 2 tbsp olive oil
- Salt and black pepper to taste

Instructions:

1. Toss vegetables with olive oil, salt, and pepper. Roast at 400°F (200°C) for 25 minutes.
2. Mix maple syrup, mustard, and soy sauce. Brush over salmon fillets.
3. Place salmon on a lined baking sheet and bake for 12-15 minutes. Serve with roasted vegetables.

Herb-Crusted Prime Rib with Au Jus

Ingredients:

- 1 (5 lb) prime rib roast
- 2 tbsp olive oil
- 1 tbsp sea salt
- 1 tbsp black pepper
- 1 tbsp fresh rosemary, chopped
- 1 tbsp fresh thyme, chopped

Au Jus:

- 1 cup beef broth
- 1/2 cup red wine

Instructions:

1. Rub roast with olive oil, salt, pepper, rosemary, and thyme. Let sit at room temperature for 1 hour.
2. Roast at 450°F (230°C) for 20 minutes, then lower to 325°F (160°C) and cook until internal temperature reaches 130°F (54°C) for medium-rare.
3. Let rest for 20 minutes.
4. Simmer beef broth and red wine in a pan, scraping up browned bits. Serve au jus with sliced roast.

Truffle Butter Filet Mignon

Ingredients:

- 2 filet mignon steaks
- 1 tbsp olive oil
- Salt and black pepper to taste
- 2 tbsp truffle butter

Instructions:

1. Heat a cast-iron skillet over high heat.
2. Season steaks with salt and pepper, then sear for 3 minutes per side.
3. Reduce heat and add truffle butter, basting steaks for 1 minute.
4. Let rest before serving.

Bison Meatloaf with Garlic Mashed Potatoes

Ingredients:

Meatloaf:

- 1 lb ground bison
- 1/2 cup breadcrumbs
- 1 egg
- 1/4 cup ketchup
- 1 tbsp Worcestershire sauce
- 1 tsp garlic powder

Mashed Potatoes:

- 2 lbs Yukon Gold potatoes
- 4 tbsp butter
- 1/2 cup heavy cream
- 3 cloves garlic, minced

Instructions:

1. Mix meatloaf ingredients and form into a loaf. Bake at 375°F (190°C) for 45 minutes.
2. Boil potatoes until tender, then mash with butter, cream, and garlic.
3. Serve sliced meatloaf with mashed potatoes.

Lobster Mac and Cheese

Ingredients:

- 2 cups cooked lobster meat, chopped
- 12 oz elbow macaroni
- 2 cups cheddar cheese, shredded
- 1 cup gruyère cheese, shredded
- 2 cups milk
- 2 tbsp butter
- 2 tbsp flour
- 1/2 tsp paprika

Instructions:

1. Cook macaroni and set aside.
2. Melt butter in a saucepan, whisk in flour, and cook for 1 minute. Gradually add milk, stirring until thickened.
3. Add cheeses and paprika, stirring until melted.
4. Stir in lobster and macaroni, then serve warm.

Coq au Vin with Root Vegetables

Ingredients:

- 4 bone-in chicken thighs
- 1 cup red wine
- 1/2 cup chicken broth
- 2 carrots, chopped
- 1 parsnip, chopped
- 8 pearl onions
- 2 cloves garlic, minced
- 1 tsp fresh thyme
- 1 tbsp butter

Instructions:

1. Brown chicken thighs in a pan. Remove and set aside.
2. Sauté garlic, carrots, parsnip, and onions in butter.
3. Add wine, broth, and thyme. Return chicken to pan and simmer for 45 minutes.
4. Serve warm.

Wild Mushroom Risotto with Parmesan

Ingredients:

- 1 1/2 cups Arborio rice
- 4 cups chicken broth, warmed
- 1 cup mixed wild mushrooms, sliced
- 1/2 cup Parmesan cheese, grated
- 1/2 cup white wine
- 2 tbsp butter
- 1 shallot, minced

Instructions:

1. Sauté shallot and mushrooms in butter. Add rice and cook for 1 minute.
2. Pour in wine and stir until absorbed.
3. Gradually add broth, stirring continuously.
4. When rice is creamy, stir in Parmesan and serve.

Braised Short Ribs with Red Wine Reduction

Ingredients:

- 4 beef short ribs
- 1 cup red wine
- 2 cups beef broth
- 1 onion, chopped
- 2 carrots, chopped
- 3 cloves garlic, minced
- 1 tbsp tomato paste

Instructions:

1. Brown short ribs in a Dutch oven. Remove and set aside.
2. Sauté onion, carrots, and garlic. Stir in tomato paste.
3. Add wine and broth, bring to a simmer. Return ribs to pot.
4. Cover and bake at 325°F (160°C) for 3 hours.

Roasted Duck with Orange Glaze

Ingredients:

- 1 whole duck
- 1/2 cup orange juice
- 1/4 cup honey
- 1 tbsp soy sauce
- 1 tsp orange zest

Instructions:

1. Score duck skin and season with salt and pepper.
2. Roast at 350°F (175°C) for 1.5 hours, basting occasionally.
3. Mix orange juice, honey, soy sauce, and zest. Brush orto duck in the last 20 minutes.
4. Let rest before carving.

Garlic Butter Tomahawk Steak

Ingredients:

- 1 tomahawk steak
- 2 tbsp olive oil
- 2 tbsp butter
- 3 cloves garlic, minced
- 1 sprig rosemary
- Salt and black pepper to taste

Instructions:

1. Season steak with salt and pepper, then sear over high heat for 2 minutes per side.
2. Transfer to a 375°F (190°C) oven and cook until internal temp reaches 130°F (54°C) for medium-rare.
3. In a pan, melt butter, add garlic and rosemary, then baste steak for 1 minute.
4. Let rest before slicing.

Seafood Chowder with Crispy Bacon

Ingredients:

- 4 slices bacon, chopped
- 1 small onion, diced
- 2 cloves garlic, minced
- 1 cup potatoes, diced
- 1/2 cup carrots, diced
- 3 cups seafood broth
- 1 cup heavy cream
- 1/2 lb shrimp, peeled
- 1/2 lb white fish, cubed
- 1/2 cup corn
- 1 tsp fresh thyme
- Salt and black pepper to taste

Instructions:

1. Cook bacon in a pot until crispy. Remove and set aside.
2. In the same pot, sauté onion, garlic, potatoes, and carrots until softened.
3. Add seafood broth and bring to a simmer for 10 minutes.
4. Stir in cream, shrimp, fish, corn, and thyme. Cook until seafood is tender.
5. Season with salt and pepper, then top with crispy bacon before serving.

Smoked Brisket with Maple Bourbon Glaze

Ingredients:

- 5 lb beef brisket
- 2 tbsp salt
- 1 tbsp black pepper
- 1 tbsp smoked paprika

Glaze:

- 1/4 cup pure maple syrup
- 1/4 cup bourbon
- 2 tbsp Dijon mustard

Instructions:

1. Rub brisket with salt, pepper, and paprika. Let sit overnight.
2. Smoke at 225°F (110°C) for 6-8 hours until tender.
3. In a saucepan, combine maple syrup, bourbon, and Dijon. Simmer for 5 minutes.
4. Brush glaze onto brisket in the last 30 minutes of cooking.
5. Rest before slicing.

Classic Chicken Cordon Bleu

Ingredients:

- 2 chicken breasts
- 4 slices ham
- 4 slices Swiss cheese
- 1/2 cup flour
- 1 egg, beaten
- 1 cup breadcrumbs
- 1 tbsp butter

Instructions:

1. Pound chicken breasts thin, then layer ham and cheese inside. Roll tightly.
2. Dredge in flour, dip in egg, then coat with breadcrumbs.
3. Heat butter in a skillet and brown chicken on all sides.
4. Bake at 375°F (190°C) for 20 minutes.

Herb-Roasted Rack of Lamb

Ingredients:

- 1 rack of lamb
- 2 tbsp olive oil
- 1 tbsp fresh rosemary, chopped
- 1 tbsp fresh thyme, chopped
- 2 cloves garlic, minced
- Salt and black pepper to taste

Instructions:

1. Mix olive oil, rosemary, thyme, and garlic. Rub onto lamb.
2. Let sit at room temperature for 30 minutes.
3. Roast at 400°F (200°C) for 20-25 minutes for medium-rare.
4. Rest before slicing.

Stuffed Pork Tenderloin with Apple and Cranberries

Ingredients:

- 1 pork tenderloin
- 1/2 cup apples, diced
- 1/4 cup dried cranberries
- 1/4 cup pecans, chopped
- 1 tsp cinnamon
- 1 tbsp maple syrup

Instructions:

1. Butterfly pork tenderloin and flatten slightly.
2. Mix apples, cranberries, pecans, cinnamon, and maple syrup. Spread inside pork.
3. Roll and tie with kitchen twine.
4. Roast at 375°F (190°C) for 30 minutes.

Honey Dijon Glazed Ham

Ingredients:

- 1 (5 lb) bone-in ham
- 1/4 cup honey
- 2 tbsp Dijon mustard
- 1 tbsp apple cider vinegar

Instructions:

1. Score ham in a diamond pattern.
2. Mix honey, Dijon, and vinegar. Brush over ham.
3. Bake at 325°F (160°C) for 1.5-2 hours, basting every 30 minutes.

Shrimp Scampi with Lemon Garlic Butter

Ingredients:

- 1 lb shrimp, peeled
- 3 tbsp butter
- 3 cloves garlic, minced
- 1/4 cup white wine
- 1 tbsp lemon juice
- 1 tbsp fresh parsley

Instructions:

1. Melt butter in a skillet, sauté garlic until fragrant.
2. Add shrimp and cook for 2 minutes per side.
3. Pour in wine and lemon juice. Simmer for 2 minutes.
4. Sprinkle with parsley and serve over pasta or rice.

Slow-Cooked Osso Buco

Ingredients:

- 4 veal shanks
- 1/2 cup flour
- 2 tbsp olive oil
- 1 onion, chopped
- 2 carrots, chopped
- 2 cloves garlic, minced
- 1 cup red wine
- 2 cups beef broth
- 1 tbsp tomato paste
- 1 tsp fresh thyme

Instructions:

1. Dredge veal shanks in flour, then sear in olive oil until browned. Remove and set aside.
2. Sauté onion, carrots, and garlic. Stir in tomato paste.
3. Pour in wine and broth. Return veal to pot.
4. Cover and simmer for 2-3 hours until tender.

BBQ Glazed Meatloaf with Sweet Potato Mash

Ingredients:

Meatloaf:

- 1 lb ground beef
- 1/2 cup breadcrumbs
- 1 egg
- 1/4 cup BBQ sauce
- 1 tbsp Worcestershire sauce

Sweet Potato Mash:

- 2 large sweet potatoes, peeled and diced
- 2 tbsp butter
- 1/4 cup milk

Instructions:

1. Mix meatloaf ingredients and shape into a loaf. Bake at 375°F (190°C) for 40 minutes.
2. Boil sweet potatoes until soft, then mash with butter and milk.
3. Brush meatloaf with extra BBQ sauce in the last 10 minutes.
4. Serve with mashed sweet potatoes.

Canadian Lobster Tail with Garlic Butter

Ingredients:

- 2 lobster tails
- 3 tbsp butter, melted
- 1 clove garlic, minced
- 1 tbsp lemon juice

Instructions:

1. Cut lobster tails down the center and pull the meat slightly out.
2. Mix butter, garlic, and lemon juice. Brush over lobster.
3. Broil for 8-10 minutes until opaque.

Stuffed Bell Peppers with Beef and Wild Rice

Ingredients:

- 4 large bell peppers, tops removed and seeds cleaned
- 1/2 lb ground beef
- 1 cup cooked wild rice
- 1/2 cup diced tomatoes
- 1/2 small onion, chopped
- 1 clove garlic, minced
- 1/2 tsp salt
- 1/2 tsp black pepper
- 1/2 cup shredded cheddar cheese

Instructions:

1. Preheat oven to 375°F (190°C).
2. In a skillet, cook beef, onion, and garlic until browned.
3. Stir in cooked wild rice, tomatoes, salt, and pepper.
4. Stuff mixture into bell peppers and place in a baking dish.
5. Cover with foil and bake for 30 minutes. Remove foil, top with cheese, and bake for 10 more minutes.

Spaghetti Carbonara with Pancetta

Ingredients:

- 12 oz spaghetti
- 4 oz pancetta, diced
- 2 eggs
- 1/2 cup grated Parmesan cheese
- 1/2 tsp black pepper
- 1 clove garlic, minced

Instructions:

1. Cook spaghetti until al dente. Reserve 1/2 cup pasta water.
2. In a skillet, cook pancetta until crispy. Add garlic and sauté for 30 seconds.
3. In a bowl, whisk eggs, Parmesan, and black pepper.
4. Toss hot pasta with pancetta, then quickly mix in egg mixture, adding pasta water if needed for creaminess.

Buttermilk Fried Chicken with Biscuits

Ingredients:

Chicken:

- 4 bone-in chicken thighs
- 1 cup buttermilk
- 1 cup all-purpose flour
- 1 tsp paprika
- 1/2 tsp salt
- 1/2 tsp black pepper
- Oil for frying

Biscuits:

- 2 cups flour
- 1 tbsp baking powder
- 1/2 tsp salt
- 1/2 cup butter, cold and cubed
- 3/4 cup buttermilk

Instructions:

1. Marinate chicken in buttermilk for at least 1 hour.
2. Mix flour, paprika, salt, and pepper. Dredge chicken in flour mixture.
3. Fry at 350°F (175°C) for 10-12 minutes until crispy.
4. For biscuits, mix dry ingredients, cut in butter, and stir in buttermilk.
5. Bake at 400°F (200°C) for 15 minutes.

Classic Chicken Alfredo

Ingredients:

- 2 chicken breasts, sliced
- 12 oz fettuccine
- 2 tbsp butter
- 2 cloves garlic, minced
- 1 cup heavy cream
- 1/2 cup grated Parmesan cheese
- 1/2 tsp black pepper

Instructions:

1. Cook fettuccine until al dente.
2. In a skillet, cook chicken until golden. Remove and set aside.
3. Melt butter, add garlic, then stir in cream and Parmesan. Simmer until thickened.
4. Toss pasta and chicken in sauce before serving.

Maple-Dijon Glazed Salmon

Ingredients:

- 4 salmon fillets
- 1/4 cup pure maple syrup
- 2 tbsp Dijon mustard
- 1 tbsp soy sauce

Instructions:

1. Preheat oven to 400°F (200°C).
2. Whisk maple syrup, Dijon, and soy sauce. Brush over salmon.
3. Bake for 12-15 minutes until flaky.

Slow-Braised Lamb Shanks

Ingredients:

- 2 lamb shanks
- 1 onion, chopped
- 2 carrots, chopped
- 3 cloves garlic, minced
- 1 cup red wine
- 2 cups beef broth
- 1 tsp rosemary

Instructions:

1. Sear lamb shanks in a pot. Remove and set aside.
2. Sauté onions, carrots, and garlic. Stir in wine and broth.
3. Return lamb to pot, cover, and braise at 325°F (160°C) for 2.5 hours.

Pecan-Crusted Trout with Brown Butter

Ingredients:

- 2 trout fillets
- 1/2 cup pecans, finely chopped
- 1/4 cup breadcrumbs
- 1/2 tsp salt
- 1 egg, beaten
- 2 tbsp butter

Instructions:

1. Mix pecans, breadcrumbs, and salt. Dip trout in egg, then coat with pecan mixture.
2. Cook in a skillet over medium heat for 3-4 minutes per side.
3. Melt butter in a pan until browned, then drizzle over trout before serving.

Seared Scallops with Lemon Butter Sauce

Ingredients:

- 12 sea scallops
- 1 tbsp olive oil
- 2 tbsp butter
- 1 tbsp lemon juice
- 1 clove garlic, minced

Instructions:

1. Heat oil in a pan over high heat. Sear scallops for 2 minutes per side. Remove.
2. In the same pan, melt butter, add garlic and lemon juice. Pour over scallops before serving.

New York Strip Steak with Blue Cheese Butter

Ingredients:

- 2 New York strip steaks
- 1 tbsp olive oil
- Salt and black pepper to taste

Blue Cheese Butter:

- 2 tbsp butter, softened
- 2 tbsp crumbled blue cheese

Instructions:

1. Season steaks with salt and pepper. Grill for 4-5 minutes per side.
2. Mix butter and blue cheese.
3. Rest steaks and top with blue cheese butter before serving.

Cajun Blackened Red Snapper

Ingredients:

- 2 red snapper fillets
- 1 tbsp Cajun seasoning
- 1 tbsp olive oil

Instructions:

1. Rub fillets with Cajun seasoning.
2. Heat oil in a skillet over high heat. Sear snapper for 3 minutes per side.

Creamy Tuscan Chicken with Sun-Dried Tomatoes

Ingredients:

- 2 chicken breasts
- 1 tbsp olive oil
- 2 cloves garlic, minced
- 1/2 cup sun-dried tomatoes, chopped
- 1 cup heavy cream
- 1/2 cup grated Parmesan cheese
- 1 cup spinach
- 1/2 tsp red pepper flakes
- Salt and black pepper to taste

Instructions:

1. Heat olive oil in a pan and sear chicken for 5 minutes per side. Remove and set aside.
2. Sauté garlic and sun-dried tomatoes for 1 minute.
3. Stir in heavy cream, Parmesan, red pepper flakes, and spinach. Simmer for 3 minutes.
4. Return chicken to pan and cook for 5 more minutes.

Wild Boar Ragu with Pappardelle

Ingredients:

- 1 lb wild boar shoulder, cubed
- 1 small onion, chopped
- 2 cloves garlic, minced
- 1 cup red wine
- 2 cups crushed tomatoes
- 1 tsp rosemary
- 1 tsp thyme
- 1/2 tsp salt
- 1/2 tsp black pepper
- 12 oz pappardelle pasta

Instructions:

1. Sear wild boar in a pan until browned. Remove and set aside.
2. Sauté onion and garlic, then deglaze with red wine.
3. Add tomatoes, herbs, salt, and pepper. Return boar to pot and simmer for 2 hours.
4. Cook pappardelle and toss with ragu before serving.

Bacon-Wrapped Filet Mignon

Ingredients:

- 2 filet mignon steaks
- 2 slices thick-cut bacon
- 1 tbsp olive oil
- Salt and black pepper to taste

Instructions:

1. Wrap bacon around each filet and secure with toothpicks.
2. Season steaks with salt and pepper.
3. Sear steaks for 2 minutes per side, then transfer to a 400°F (200°C) oven for 6-8 minutes for medium-rare.
4. Rest for 5 minutes before serving.

Garlic Butter Lobster Tails with Parmesan Asparagus

Ingredients:

- 2 lobster tails
- 3 tbsp butter, melted
- 2 cloves garlic, minced
- 1 tbsp lemon juice

Parmesan Asparagus:

- 1 bunch asparagus
- 1 tbsp olive oil
- 1/4 cup grated Parmesan
- Salt and black pepper to taste

Instructions:

1. Preheat oven to 400°F (200°C).
2. Cut lobster shells and pull meat slightly out. Mix butter, garlic, and lemon juice, then brush onto lobster.
3. Roast lobster tails for 10-12 minutes.
4. Toss asparagus with olive oil and season with salt and pepper. Roast for 10 minutes, then sprinkle with Parmesan.

Pan-Seared Duck Breast with Cherry Sauce

Ingredients:

- 2 duck breasts
- 1/2 cup cherries, pitted and halved
- 1/4 cup red wine
- 1 tbsp honey
- 1 tsp balsamic vinegar

Instructions:

1. Score duck skin and season with salt and pepper.
2. Sear skin-side down in a cold pan for 6 minutes, then flip and cook for 4 more minutes. Rest before slicing.
3. In the same pan, add cherries, wine, honey, and vinegar. Simmer for 5 minutes.
4. Spoon cherry sauce over sliced duck breast.

Roast Chicken with Lemon and Thyme

Ingredients:

- 1 whole chicken
- 1 lemon, halved
- 2 tbsp butter, melted
- 2 tsp fresh thyme
- Salt and black pepper to taste

Instructions:

1. Preheat oven to 375°F (190°C).
2. Rub chicken with butter, salt, pepper, and thyme. Place lemon halves inside the cavity.
3. Roast for 1 hour 20 minutes, basting occasionally.
4. Let rest for 10 minutes before carving.

Seafood Paella with Saffron Rice

Ingredients:

- 1 cup Arborio or paella rice
- 2 cups seafood broth
- 1/2 tsp saffron threads
- 1/2 lb shrimp
- 1/2 lb mussels
- 1/2 lb calamari
- 1 tomato, chopped
- 1 small onion, chopped
- 2 cloves garlic, minced
- 1/2 tsp smoked paprika

Instructions:

1. Heat oil in a pan and sauté onion, garlic, and tomato.
2. Stir in rice, saffron, and smoked paprika. Add broth and simmer for 15 minutes.
3. Add seafood and cook for another 5-7 minutes until mussels open.

Classic Shepherd's Pie

Ingredients:

- 1 lb ground lamb or beef
- 1 small onion, chopped
- 2 carrots, diced
- 1/2 cup peas
- 2 tbsp tomato paste
- 1 cup beef broth
- 2 lbs mashed potatoes
- 2 tbsp butter

Instructions:

1. Brown meat with onion and carrots. Stir in tomato paste and broth. Simmer for 10 minutes.
2. Spread into a baking dish, top with mashed potatoes, and dot with butter.
3. Bake at 375°F (190°C) for 25 minutes.

Moroccan Spiced Lamb Chops

Ingredients:

- 4 lamb chops
- 1 tsp ground cumin
- 1 tsp ground coriander
- 1/2 tsp cinnamon
- 1/2 tsp paprika
- 1 tbsp olive oil

Instructions:

1. Mix spices with olive oil and rub onto lamb chops.
2. Let marinate for 30 minutes.
3. Sear lamb for 3-4 minutes per side.
4. Rest for 5 minutes before serving.

Stuffed Shells with Ricotta and Spinach

Ingredients:

- 12 jumbo pasta shells
- 1 cup ricotta cheese
- 1/2 cup mozzarella, shredded
- 1/2 cup spinach, chopped
- 1 egg
- 1/2 tsp salt
- 1/2 tsp black pepper
- 2 cups marinara sauce

Instructions:

1. Cook pasta shells and set aside.
2. Mix ricotta, mozzarella, spinach, egg, salt, and pepper.
3. Stuff shells with mixture and place in a baking dish with marinara sauce.
4. Bake at 375°F (190°C) for 20 minutes.

Sweet and Sour Glazed Pork Chops

Ingredients:

- 2 pork chops
- 1/4 cup brown sugar
- 2 tbsp apple cider vinegar
- 1 tbsp soy sauce
- 1 tsp garlic powder

Instructions:

1. Season pork chops with salt and pepper.
2. Sear in a pan for 3 minutes per side.
3. In a saucepan, mix brown sugar, vinegar, soy sauce, and garlic powder. Simmer for 3 minutes.
4. Brush glaze over pork chops and cook for another 3 minutes.

Blackened Cajun Salmon with Avocado Salsa

Ingredients:

Salmon:

- 4 salmon fillets
- 1 tbsp olive oil
- 1 tbsp Cajun seasoning
- 1/2 tsp smoked paprika
- 1/2 tsp salt

Avocado Salsa:

- 1 avocado, diced
- 1/2 cup cherry tomatoes, diced
- 1/4 cup red onion, finely chopped
- 1 tbsp lime juice
- 1 tbsp cilantro, chopped
- Salt and pepper to taste

Instructions:

1. Rub salmon with olive oil, Cajun seasoning, paprika, and salt.
2. Heat a skillet over medium-high heat and sear salmon for 3-4 minutes per side.
3. Mix salsa ingredients in a bowl.
4. Serve salmon topped with avocado salsa.

Chicken Marsala with Creamy Mushroom Sauce

Ingredients:

- 2 chicken breasts, pounded thin
- 1/2 cup flour
- 1/2 tsp salt
- 1/2 tsp black pepper
- 2 tbsp butter
- 1 cup mushrooms, sliced
- 1/2 cup Marsala wine
- 1/2 cup chicken broth
- 1/4 cup heavy cream

Instructions:

1. Coat chicken in flour, salt, and pepper.
2. Heat butter in a pan and cook chicken for 4 minutes per side. Remove and set aside.
3. Sauté mushrooms, then deglaze with Marsala wine. Stir in broth and cream.
4. Return chicken to pan and simmer for 5 minutes.

Roasted Turkey with Cranberry Sauce

Ingredients:

Turkey:

- 1 (10-12 lb) turkey
- 1/4 cup butter, melted
- 1 tsp salt
- 1/2 tsp black pepper
- 1 tsp fresh thyme

Cranberry Sauce:

- 2 cups fresh cranberries
- 1/2 cup sugar
- 1/2 cup orange juice

Instructions:

1. Rub turkey with butter, salt, pepper, and thyme. Roast at 325°F (165°C) for 3-4 hours.
2. For cranberry sauce, simmer cranberries, sugar, and orange juice for 10 minutes.
3. Let turkey rest before slicing and serve with cranberry sauce.

Prime Rib with Horseradish Cream Sauce

Ingredients:

Prime Rib:

- 1 (5 lb) prime rib roast
- 2 tbsp olive oil
- 2 tsp salt
- 1 tsp black pepper
- 1 tsp garlic powder

Horseradish Cream Sauce:

- 1/2 cup sour cream
- 2 tbsp prepared horseradish
- 1 tsp lemon juice
- Salt and pepper to taste

Instructions:

1. Rub roast with olive oil, salt, pepper, and garlic powder. Let sit for 1 hour.
2. Roast at 450°F (230°C) for 20 minutes, then reduce to 325°F (165°C) and cook until internal temp reaches 130°F (54°C).
3. Mix horseradish sauce ingredients and serve with sliced prime rib.

Creamy Lobster Bisque

Ingredients:

- 2 lobster tails
- 2 tbsp butter
- 1 small onion, chopped
- 1 clove garlic, minced
- 1/4 cup white wine
- 2 cups seafood broth
- 1/2 cup heavy cream
- 1/2 tsp paprika

Instructions:

1. Steam lobster tails, remove meat, and chop. Save shells.
2. Sauté onion and garlic in butter. Add lobster shells and cook for 5 minutes.
3. Pour in wine and seafood broth, simmer for 20 minutes, then strain.
4. Stir in cream, paprika, and lobster meat. Simmer for 5 more minutes before serving.

Beef Stroganoff with Egg Noodles

Ingredients:

- 1 lb beef sirloin, sliced
- 1/2 tsp salt
- 1/2 tsp black pepper
- 2 tbsp butter
- 1 small onion, chopped
- 1 cup mushrooms, sliced
- 1/2 cup beef broth
- 1/2 cup sour cream
- 12 oz egg noodles

Instructions:

1. Cook egg noodles and set aside.
2. Season beef with salt and pepper. Sear in butter for 2 minutes per side. Remove
3. Sauté onions and mushrooms. Add beef broth and simmer.
4. Stir in sour cream and return beef to pan. Serve over egg noodles.

Maple Glazed Duck Confit

Ingredients:

- 2 duck legs
- 1 tsp salt
- 1/2 tsp black pepper
- 1 tsp fresh thyme
- 1/4 cup pure maple syrup

Instructions:

1. Season duck legs with salt, pepper, and thyme.
2. Place in a baking dish and slow-roast at 250°F (120°C) for 2.5 hours.
3. Brush with maple syrup and broil for 5 minutes until crispy.

Lemon Garlic Shrimp Risotto

Ingredients:

- 1 cup Arborio rice
- 4 cups chicken broth, warmed
- 1/2 lb shrimp, peeled
- 2 tbsp butter
- 1 clove garlic, minced
- 1/4 cup white wine
- 1 tbsp lemon juice
- 1/4 cup grated Parmesan

Instructions:

1. Sauté shrimp in butter with garlic for 2 minutes. Remove and set aside.
2. In the same pan, add rice and toast for 1 minute.
3. Pour in white wine and stir until absorbed.
4. Add warm broth, one ladle at a time, stirring until absorbed before adding more.
5. When rice is creamy, stir in shrimp, lemon juice, and Parmesan before serving.